Across the Curriculum: Curriculum: SCIENCE for ages 10–11

A wide range of teachers' notes and photocopiable worksheets to address the needs of teachers and children in covering several aspects of the curriculum, while learning valuable concepts in science.

Across the Curriculum: Science for ages 10–11

Contents

Across the Curriculum: Science for ages 10–11

We show possible curriculum links but we will not have thought of everything so you may like to add some of your own.

Literacy

Vocabulary.
Use of keys to identify
animals and plants.
Revision of previous work:
What do plants need to grow well?
Creating information sheets about
animals or plants.
Summarising texts.
Retrieving information from texts.

Art

Observational drawings of
plants and their roots.

IT

Writing information
sheets on specific
animals or plants.

Interdependence

and

Adaptation

Numeracy

Use of keys to
identify organisms.

Worksheets 1 to 4 all contain descriptions of organisms. They have been written in order to be accessible to most Year 6 children.

Worksheet 1 concerns the Red Admiral butterfly. Children may need reminding of the stages in the life cycle of butterflies and moths, particularly the metamorphic process of changes in form from caterpillar to adult. The Red Admiral migrates to Northern Europe from the Mediterranean, to reproduce. In the autumn some of the adults die but others migrate back to the Mediterranean. To introduce principles of classification of organisms we show the kingdom, phylum, class, order and species. Children can be encouraged to use dictionaries to find out the meanings of 'phylum' and 'arthropod'. They can also use CD Roms or reference books to look up the Red Admiral to find pictures showing colours.

Worksheet 2 features information on the Little Owl, a bird that was introduced to Britain at the end of the nineteenth century and is now fairly widespread.

Worksheet 3 provides information on the Wood Mushroom. This mushroom is an edible variety. We strongly suggest that children do not touch mushrooms apart from those purchased in a food store and that they are informed, very clearly, that some mushrooms are very poisonous. The Worksheet states that the mushroom appears in the autumn, though the fungus itself is present in the soil all year round.

Worksheet 4 is different to the previous three in that it concerns a cultivated plant, the Iceberg rose, and provides information for gardeners regarding how to plant it and keep it healthy.

Worksheets 5 and 6 provide questions related to the four information sheets. Questions 2, 3 and 4 on Worksheet 5 all concern Worksheet 4. For question 3 the children should be able to identify that Worksheet 4 does not have a heading, 'recognition'. For question 4 they should be able to state that Worksheet 4 is designed to give information to gardeners whereas the other sheets provide information regarding the natural occurrence of each species. On Worksheet 6, question 7 requires an answer that demonstrates that children know plants can benefit from nutrients gained through the soil.

Worksheet 7 is designed to test children's previous knowledge of food chains, ensuring that they use the correct technical vocabulary.

Children should use ideas from Worksheets 1 to 4 to assist them in creating an information sheet on Worksheet 8. They need to decide whether this will be an instructional sheet for gardeners or an identification and guidance sheet similar to Worksheets 1 to 3.

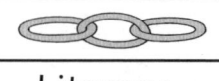
Name: Date:

The Red Admiral

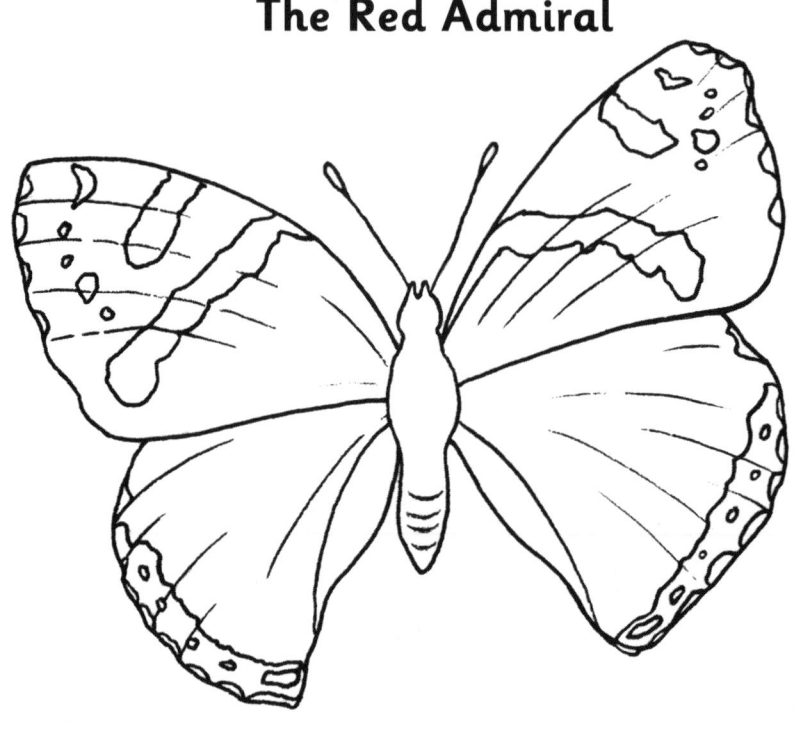

Kingdom :	animals
Phylum:	arthropods
Class:	insects
Order:	butterflies and moths
Species:	Red Admiral

Recognition: The adult measures approximately 6–7 cm across the wingspan. Colouring is predominantly dark brown with some white patches at the points of the front wings, and distinctive red stripes across the front pair of wings and along the outside edges of the rear wings.

Extent: North Africa, Europe, Western Asia, North America, Central America. Migrates to Britain from the Mediterranean for the summer months.

Present: May to October. Caterpillar form from May to September.

Food: Stinging nettles; ripe fruits including apples and plums.

Habitat: Woodland edges, gardens, orchards.

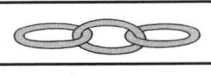
Name:

Date:

The Little Owl

Kingdom :	animals
Phylum:	chordates
Sub-Phylum:	vertebrates
Class:	bird
Species:	Little Owl

Recognition: The adult measures approximately 21cm in height.
The plumage is brown, mottled with white.
The wings are short and rounded.

Extent: Europe, Central Asia, North Africa.

Present: All year.

Food: Insects; small mammals.

Habitat: Open countryside; lightly wooded areas.

Nesting: Holes in trees, walls and old rabbit burrows.

Eggs: April – May; 3 – 5; white.

Name: Date:

The Wood Mushroom

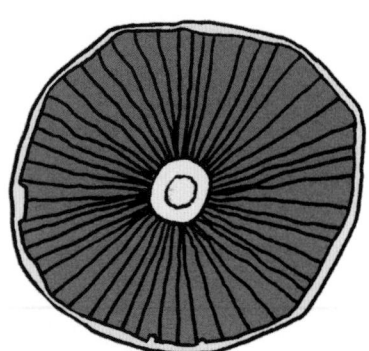

Kingdom :	fungi
Phylum:	basidiomycetes
Class:	mushrooms
Species:	Wood Mushroom

Recognition: Cap is 5 – 10cm diameter.
Colour is creamy white or yellow.
Stem: 5 – 8cm tall.
Gills: pale pink at first, becoming brown later.

Present: The mushroom appears in the autumn.

Habitat: Woodland.

 Be careful. Do not touch mushrooms or other fungi without adult help.
Some mushrooms and other fungi are poisonous and can be fatal.

Using the information provided, label the picture of the mushroom.

Name: Date:

The Iceberg Rose

Height:	24″/60cm
Spacing:	30″/75cm
Flowering:	July/August
Cultivation:	Plant in autumn or spring.
	Good soil, well-drained.
	Add well-rotted manure or compost.
	Sun or partial shade.

Care: Prune by shortening shoots back to an outward facing bud approximately 15cm (6 inches) from the ground.

The Iceberg rose is one of our most popular garden plants. It bears abundant beautiful white flowers in the warm summer months and is a delight to all gardeners' eyes. When planted close together the bushes can make an ideal hedge.

INTERDEPENDENCE AND ADAPTATION

Literacy

Name: | Date:

Retrieving information – sheet A

Look at the four information sheets:
'The Red Admiral',   'The Little Owl',   'The Wood Mushroom' and 'The Iceberg Rose'.

1 What does 'extent' mean?

_____

_____

2 Which sheet does not have the headings 'Kingdom', 'Phylum', 'Class' and 'Species'?

_____

_____

3 How else is this sheet different from the others?

_____

_____

4 Why is this sheet different from the others?

_____

_____

5 The Red Admiral is present from May to October. What does 'present' mean?
   Where is the Red Admiral for the rest of the year?

_____

_____

6 Use the information on the sheet, together with a reference book, to colour the picture of the Red Admiral carefully and accurately.

7 Using information from reference books, draw the life cycle of the Red Admiral on the back of this sheet.

Name: Date:

Retrieving information – sheet B

Look at the four information sheets:
'The Red Admiral',   'The Little Owl',   'The Wood Mushroom' and 'The Iceberg Rose'.

1 The Red Admiral and the Little Owl are both from the animal kingdom. What kingdom does the Wood Mushroom belong to?

_____

2 What kingdom do you think the Iceberg Rose belongs to?

_____

3 What colour do you think the Iceberg Rose is?

_____

4 Which of the four sheets describes a vertebrate?

_____

5 What is a vertebrate?

_____

_____

6 Why should you be careful about mushrooms and other fungi?

_____

_____

7 Why might you add well-rotted manure or compost to the soil in which you plant the rose?

_____

_____

Name: | Date:

A food chain

Draw a food chain in the box below.

Remember that food chains start with green plants; you could start yours with a stinging nettle.

Food chains are drawn with arrows facing upwards. The green plant should be at the bottom.

Try to make your food chain have four levels. Write a short description of each level. You could include these words:

> **producer   consumer   first order (primary)**
> **predator second order (secondary)**
> **third order (tertiary)   prey.**

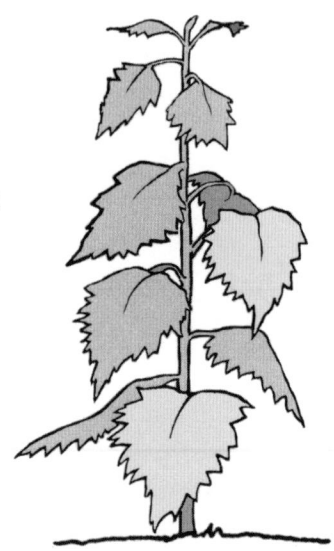

Andrew Brodie Publications © A & C Black Publishers Ltd.

Name: Date:

Write your own information sheet

Write your own information sheet for a particular organism. Draw a coloured picture of the organism and write brief descriptions under appropriate headings, for example 'recognition', 'extent', 'present', 'food', 'habitat', 'nesting', 'eggs', 'cultivation', 'care', etc.

We show possible curriculum links but we will not have thought of everything so you may like to add some of your own.

Literacy

Vocabulary.
Recognise that 'germ' is a term for micro-organism that causes disease. Retrieving information from texts: researching scientists who identified microbes as a source of some diseases. Observations and written descriptions of the use of yeast in bread making.

ICT

CD Roms: sourcing information on famous scientists.

Numeracy

Measuring the area of mould growing on bread.

History

Scientists who 'discovered' and experimented with germs.

DT

Food preservation and food hygiene. Storing food with care. (Note: mouldy food should be kept in sealed containers.)

Micro-Organisms

PSHE

Litter. Biodegradable and non-biodegradable materials.

Geography

Tour the school grounds to find natural materials that are decaying.

Worksheet 1 concerns appropriate technical vocabulary. Children are asked to use a dictionary to look up specified words, then to create a simple definition. The word 'mould' has several definitions; children need to find the one that is relevant to the topic. The word 'bacteria' is the plural form of the singular word 'bacterium'.

Worksheet 2 invites children to use reference sources to find information regarding five scientists. Possible answers are shown here:

~ Louis Pasteur 1822–1895 French. Suggested the germ theory of causes of disease. Invented pasteurisation as a method of killing micro-organisms in wine, beer and milk.
~ Robert Koch   1843–1910 German. Isolated some of the bacteria that cause diseases.
~ Edward Jenner 1749–1823 English.   Used germs from a disease called cowpox to create a vaccine against smallpox.
~ Alexander Fleming 1881–1955 Scottish. Discovered penicillin.
~ Antoni van Leeuwenhoek   1632–1723 Dutch.   First person to observe bacteria and yeast using an early form of microscope.

As a further activity the children could be asked to arrange the five scientists in historical order, perhaps using a timeline.

Worksheet 3 provides a recipe for making bread. It would be appropriate to discuss what happens at the stage when the dough is rising. Children should realise that the rising is caused by the respiration of the yeast. Stress the importance of washing hands before cooking.

Worksheet 4 refers to moulds and the dangers associated with them. Children also need to learn that some micro-organisms are useful in food production, notably that of bread, yoghurt and cheese. Clearly, safety rules must be adhered to when children complete the activity on the sheet. Note that mouldy foods should be kept in closed containers. To record their findings, children can draw the bread on the grid on Worksheet 5. They can find the approximate area of the slice of bread by counting squares, then use an estimation method to find the approximate area of mould growth. The percentage of mould growth can be found using the following formula.

$$\frac{\text{Area of mould growth}}{\text{Area of bread}} \quad \text{x } 100$$

Worksheet 6 features a chart to record the type of litter found in the school grounds according to whether it is biodegradable or non-biodegradable. The idea behind the Worksheet is to stimulate discussion regarding dropping litter and types of litter. Please note that you may need to consult local authority policy statements regarding safety of children; some local authorities advise against children collecting litter. It would be possible to complete the Worksheet, leaving the litter where it is.

MICRO-ORGANISMS

Name: _____ Date: _____

Vocabulary

Use a dictionary to find simple definitions for the words shown below. Be careful: one of the words has several meanings; choose the meaning that is relevant to this topic.

Microbe _____

_____

_____

Bacteria _____

_____

_____

Germ _____

_____

_____

Virus _____

_____

_____

Yeast _____

_____

_____

Mould _____

_____

_____

1 Which of the words has several meanings? _____

2 Which of the words is in the plural form? _____

3 What is the singular form of this word? _____

Andrew Brodie Publications © A & C Black Publishers Ltd.

Name: _____   Date: _____

Scientists

Many scientists have investigated germs, diseases caused by germs and how to cure these diseases. Using reference books or a computer find the information requested below on the following scientists: Louis Pasteur, Robert Koch, Edward Jenner, Alexander Fleming, Antoni van Leeuwenhoek.

Name: _____   Nationality: _____

Year of birth: _____   Year of death: _____

Contribution to the subject: _____

_____

_____

Name: _____   Nationality: _____

Year of birth: _____   Year of death: _____

Contribution to the subject: _____

_____

_____

Name: _____   Nationality: _____

Year of birth: _____   Year of death: _____

Contribution to the subject: _____

_____

_____

Name: _____   Nationality: _____

Year of birth: _____   Year of death: _____

Contribution to the subject: _____

_____

_____

Name: _____   Nationality: _____

Year of birth: _____   Year of death: _____

Contribution to the subject: _____

_____

_____

Name: Date:

Making bread

Ingredients
750g wholemeal flour
4 level teaspoons of salt
1 packet of easy bake yeast (7g packet)
1 tablespoon of olive oil
450ml warm water
extra olive oil
You will also need a loaf tin

Method

1 Put the flour, the salt and the yeast into a bowl.

2 Mix them together.

3 Pour in the tablespoon of olive oil and the warm water.

4 Use your hands to mix the ingredients together. When combined, they should make a big ball of soft dough.

5 Sprinkle some flour onto a flat surface.

6 Lift the dough onto the flat surface and keep turning it over and pressing into it with your fists. This is called kneading. You should knead the dough for three minutes.

7 Spread some olive oil over the inside surface of a loaf tin.

8 Put the dough into the loaf tin, then leave it in a warm place. Ask an adult to turn on the oven to gas mark 7, 220°C.

9 You should check the dough after half an hour. If it has grown to double its size it's ready to bake. If it hasn't grown, you should leave it in the warm place for longer.

10 When the dough is ready, ask an adult to put it in the oven. It will be very hot so you must have the help of an adult.

11 After 35 minutes ask an adult to put on some oven gloves and take the loaf out of the oven.

12 Leave it to cool, then take it out of the loaf tin. It is ready to eat.

Andrew Brodie Publications © A & C Black Publishers Ltd.

Name:

Date:

Mould – sheet A

There are micro-organisms in the air around us. Some of these micro-organisms can infect our food, causing us to become ill. To try to avoid such illnesses we need to follow some hygiene rules.

1 Wash hands before touching any food.

2 Store food carefully. Some food needs to be kept in a refrigerator.

3 Eat food when it is fresh.

When food is not fresh, mould sometimes grows on it.

 Eating mould can make you ill. You should always wash your hands if you touch mould or any other fungus.

Grow your own mould!

You are going to keep a slice of bread in conditions that will encourage mould to grow. Mould will grow well in warm and damp conditions, similar to some of those needed by plants.

You will need:
~ a slice of bread
~ a clear plastic bag
~ a warm place

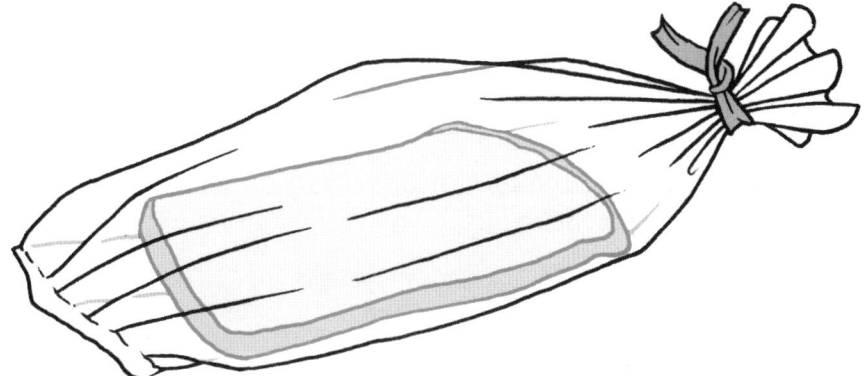

Sprinkle the bread with a small amount of water. Place the slice of bread into a clear plastic bag and tie it up; leave some air space in the bag, trying not to wrap the bread tightly in the plastic. Put the bag in a warm place. Observe the bread every day for several days. Record what you see on Worksheet 5.

Name: _____ Date: _____

Mould – sheet B

Draw your slice of bread on the grid below. Observe the bread every day. Record any mould that grows by drawing it in the correct place. Try to match the colours of the mould that you can see on your bread. After about a week, estimate what percentage of the slice of bread has mould on.

Eating mould can make you ill. You should always wash your hands if you touch mould or any other fungus.

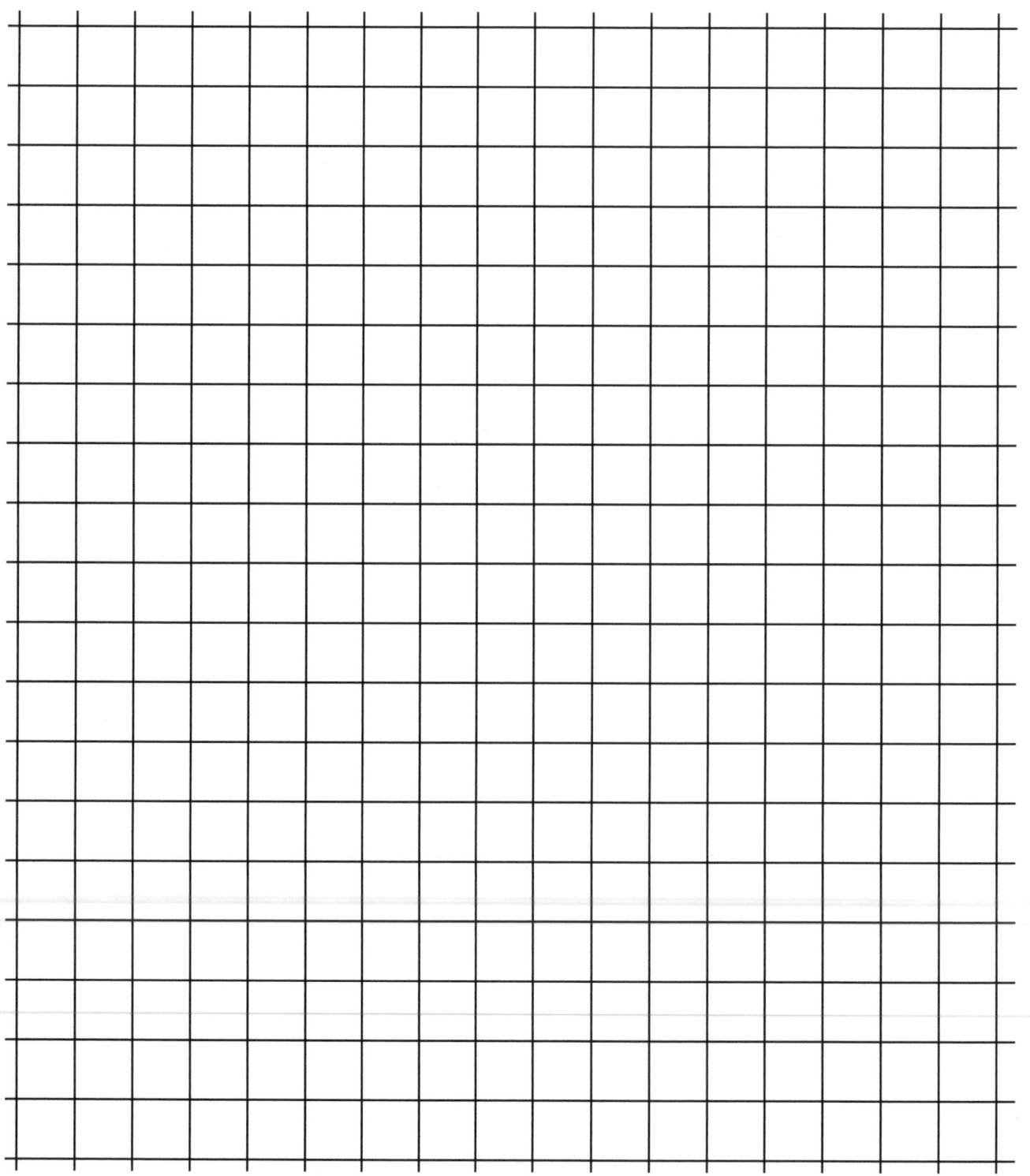

Name: | Date:

Litter

You will need:
~ plastic gloves
~ plastic bags

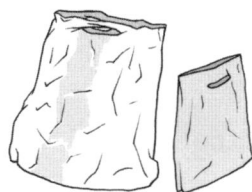

 Do not work in areas where dogs visit. Dogs' faeces contain very dangerous micro-organisms.

You are going to examine part of the school grounds for litter. Collect litter by placing it into plastic bags.

 You must wear plastic gloves when collecting the litter and you must wash your hands after the activity, to avoid being infected by any unhealthy micro-organisms.

When you return to class, complete the chart below.

Item of litter	Where found	Biodegradable – Yes ✓ – No x

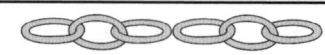
We show possible curriculum links but we will not have thought of everything so you may like to add some of your own.

Literacy

Vocabulary.
Writing a step by step description of the process of separating solids from water

by filtering.

IT

Use of spreadsheets for recording data.

Geography

Evaporation of water from the sea. Does the salt evaporate too? The water cycle.

Dissolving

Numeracy

Line graphs and their interpretation. Reading thermometers. Volumes of liquids. Measuring time. Presenting results in a table.

Worksheet 1 could be used as an assessment activity at the start of the topic, to check children's existing knowledge of processes affecting water. The solutions to the crossword puzzle are as follows.

Across: 1 condensation; 4 evaporation; 8 evaporate; 9 filter; 10 mixture
11 dissolved; 12 condense.

Down: 2 sieve; 3 undissolved; 5 pure; 6 clear; 7 solution.

Worksheets 2 and 3 are used together to create a simple diagram of the water cycle. You may prefer children to create their own picture of the water cycle, using the Worksheets to provide the key points. Understanding of the water cycle is essential before children consider the investigation contained in Worksheet 4.

Worksheet 4 provides an investigation into whether rainwater contains salt. It would be appropriate to discuss the water cycle with the children before starting the investigation. Children should be able to state that sea water is salty and that clouds form from evaporated water from the sea. The clouds bring water in the form of rain (or other precipitation) and therefore the question can be asked, 'Does rainwater contain salt?' Once the water has evaporated from the two saucers the children should be able to observe that the saucer that contained the tap water mixed with salt now contains salt crystals whereas the saucer that contained rainwater does not contain salt crystals.

Worksheet 5 describes an experiment to test whether sugar dissolves better in warm water or in cold water. Before showing the children the sheet it would be appropriate to ask for their scientific opinion on the subject. Read through the method with the children, ensuring that they understand the process that took place. The method is written in the third person and could be used as a model for children's own writing up of experiments.

Worksheet 6 contains the results of the experiment described on Worksheet 5. Children should be encouraged to predict what would have happened if the temperature of the water had been increased or, perhaps, decreased. They could extend the line on the graph to try to find accurate predictions. They could be asked to estimate the dissolving time if the temperature of the water was 15°C, 25°C, 35°C or 45°C. If children carry out the experiment themselves, care should be taken to ensure that the water temperature is not too high. Normally water from a hot tap in school should be of a safe temperature.

Name: Date:

Crossword

These words all appear on the crossword puzzle below.

evaporate   evaporation   dissolved   undissolved

solution   condense   condensation

filter   sieve   mixture   pure   clear

Use the clues to find where each word belongs.

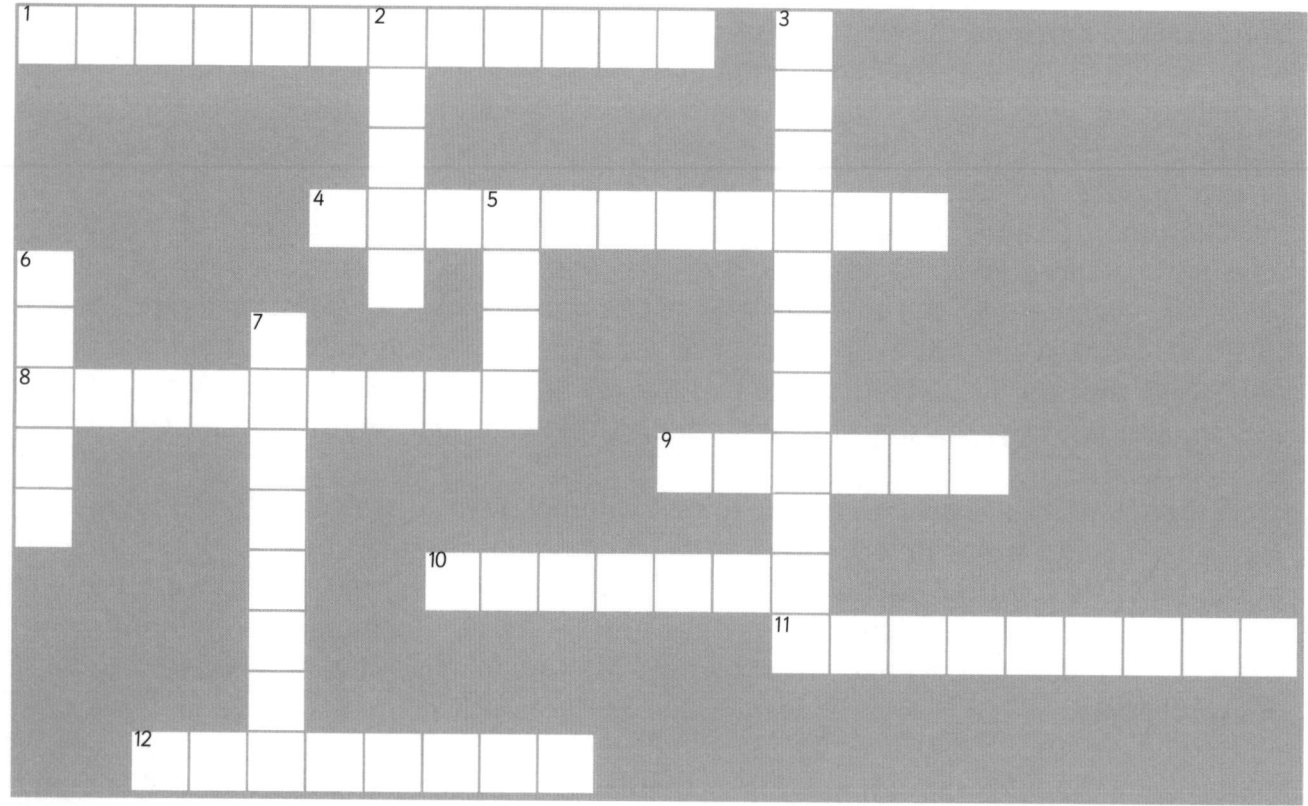

Across

1 The process of changing from a vapour to a liquid (for example, when water vapour changes to droplets of water on a cold window).

4 The process of changing from a liquid to a vapour.

8 To change from a liquid to a vapour.

9 Used to remove solid particles from a liquid.

10 Something mixed together is a _ _ _ _ _ _ _

11 In solution. (For example, sugar can be _ _ _ _ _ _ _ _ _ in a hot drink).

12 To change from a vapour to a liquid.

Down

2 A utensil for separating solids from liquids.

3 Not dissolved.

5 Unmixed.

6 Transparent.

7 A liquid containing dissolved solid material (for example, dissolving salt in water produces a salt _ _ _ _ _ _ _ _).

Name:

Date:

The Water cycle – sheet A

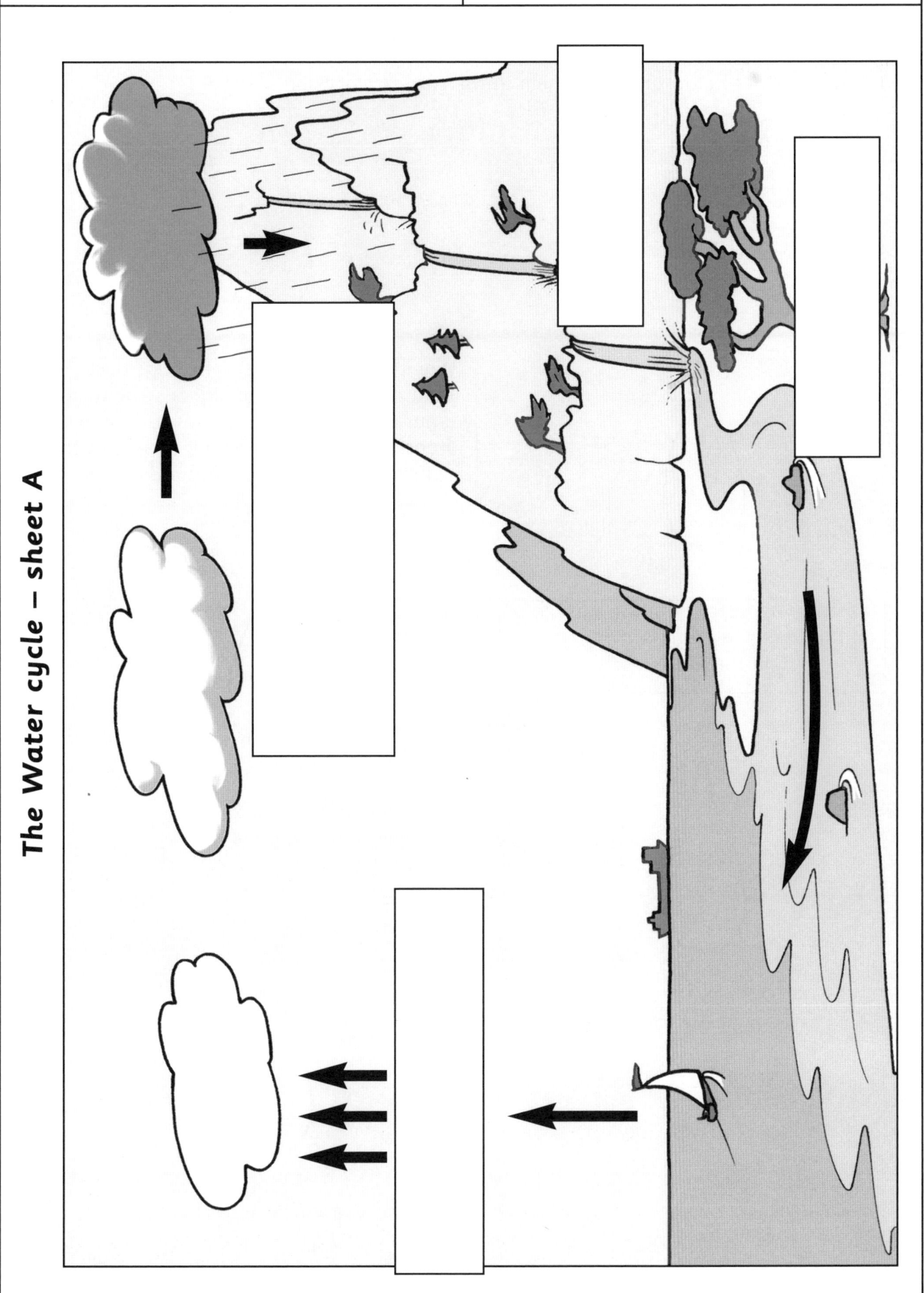

Name:

Date:

The Water cycle – sheet B

Cut out the boxes below and stick them in the correct places on Sheet A.

The water gathers in streams
and rivers, then runs back to
the sea.

When the wind blows the clouds over the
land, the clouds move higher. The water
vapour in the cloud condenses to form water
drops. These are too heavy to stay in the
air so they fall to the ground as rain.

Water evaporates from the surface
of the sea. The water vapour rises
and forms clouds.

Some of the water soaks
into the ground. Some is
used by trees and plants.

Name: | Date:

Does rainwater contain salt?

The water cycle diagram shows us that clouds are formed from water vapour that has evaporated from the sea. Sea water contains salt.
Do the clouds contain salt? Does rainwater collect salt?

You will need:
- a jar of rainwater
- a jar of tap water
- some salt
- a measuring cylinder
- two saucers

1 Pour some salt into the tap water.

2 Stir the salt and water until the salt dissolves.

3 Pour and stir more salt. Keep doing so until no more salt will dissolve.

4 Pour the salt water into a measuring cylinder, up to the 50ml mark.

5 Carefully pour the 50 millilitres of salt water into a saucer.
  Write a label saying 'salt water'.

6 Rinse out the measuring cylinder under a tap. Why?

7 Pour rainwater into the measuring cylinder, up to the 50ml mark.

8 Carefully pour the 50 millilitres of rainwater into another saucer. Write a label saying 'rainwater'.

9 Without spilling any water put the two saucers somewhere safe, to allow the water to evaporate.

10 Wait for the water to evaporate, then compare the two saucers.

salt water

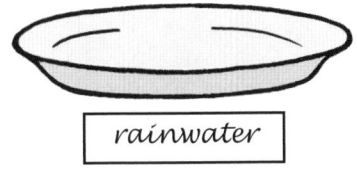

rainwater

Name:

Date:

Dissolving sugar – sheet A

An experiment to test the prediction that sugar will dissolve more quickly in hot water than in cold water.

Method

1 A measuring jug was filled to the 500ml mark with cold water from the tap. Ice was added to the water until the temperature of the water was 10°C.

2 1 teaspoon of granulated sugar was added to the water and a timer started.

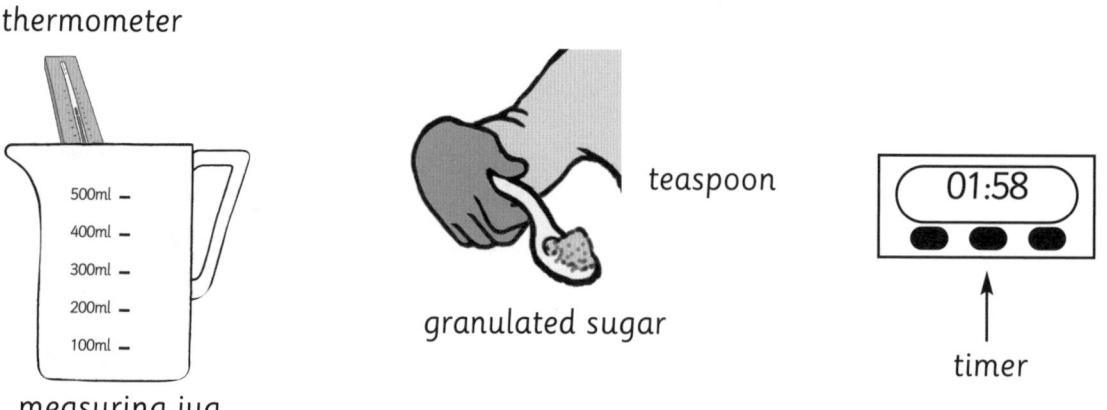

thermometer

500ml
400ml
300ml
200ml
100ml

measuring jug

teaspoon

granulated sugar

01:58

timer

Constants: 500ml water   1 teaspoon granulated sugar.

3 The water and sugar were stirred only when the sugar was first put in and again at 1 minute intervals if the sugar was not dissolved.

4 The time taken for the sugar to dissolve was noted.

5 The experiment was repeated with the water at temperatures of 20°C, 30°C, 40°C and 50°C. Hot water from the tap was added to cold tap water to obtain the correct temperature of water.

6 The results are shown on Worksheet 6.

7 A line graph of the results is also shown.

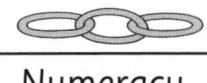
Name: Date:

Dissolving sugar – sheet B

Results

Cold water	10°C	– time taken to dissolve –	480 seconds
	20°C	– time taken to dissolve –	330 seconds
Lukewarm water	30°C	– time taken to dissolve –	180 seconds
	40°C	– time taken to dissolve –	130 seconds
Hot water	50°C	– time taken to dissolve –	90 seconds

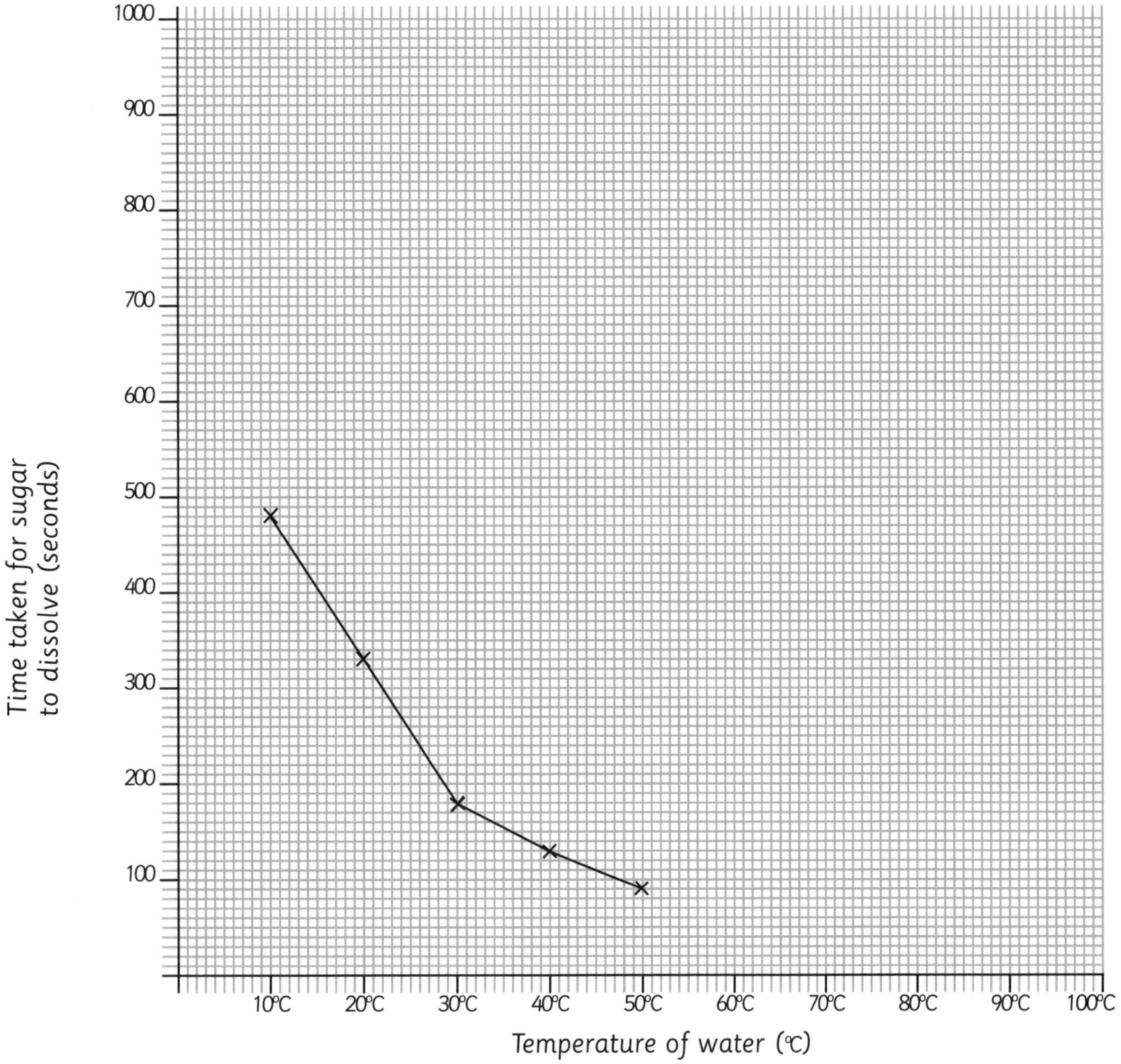

Time taken for sugar to dissolve (seconds)

Temperature of water (°C)

We show possible curriculum links but we will not have thought of everything so you may like to add some of your own.

Literacy

Vocabulary. Using word roots, prefixes and suffixes. Summarising a text in a specific number of words. Retrieving information from text. Constructing effective arguments.

DT

Mixing ingredients to make a cake: heating in oven.

Reversible and Irreversible Changes

Art

Modelling with plaster. Poster showing hazards of burning materials.

Numeracy

Measuring volumes of water. Accurate measurements of volumes and lengths.

Worksheet 1 is a combined literacy/numeracy/DT sheet. A question at the top of the page requires them to identify water vapour as the gaseous form of H_2O. Children need to read instructions, measure carefully, then create a cube-shaped box in which to make an ice cube. It is advisable to prepare the pieces of plastic beforehand by cutting squares, with sides of approximately 12cm, from thin but strong plastic bags.

Children should be encouraged to discuss the suitability of materials for this task: Why use plastic? Would cling film work? Children will probably find that the volume of water poured in does not match the capacity of the cube as the plastic will not occupy the corners, again providing an opportunity to discuss the materials used and to consider whether there would be a better way to make a cube of ice. Note that we refer to 'ice cubes' in everyday language but that these are very rarely mathematical cubes.

Worksheet 2 continues the work with the ice cube. Children should observe that the ice cube now appears to be larger than the box as water expands as it turns to ice. We would expect children to state that melting is a reversible change as we could freeze the water again. Any variations in volumes may be due to spillage.

Worksheet 3 contains vocabulary related to changes in state, particularly of H_2O. The answers to the puzzle are as follows.

     Down: 1. melting; 3. reversible; 4. freezing.
     Across: 2. evaporating; 5. irreversible; 6. condensing.

Worksheet 4 contains useful and relevant information, but also provides the opportunity for children to practise a very important skill: summarising texts. Children need to extract the key information from each of the two paragraphs provided, then write this information in a readable style but in less than 20 words.

Worksheet 5 could be used as an assessment sheet at the end of the topic. The answers are as follows.

1 reversible; 2 reversible; 3 irreversible; 4 reversible; 5 irreversible; 6 reversible.

Worksheet 6 provides an edible example of a set of irreversible changes. Children can enjoy making the cakes, while identifying each change that takes place.

Name: | **Date:**

Water and ice – sheet A

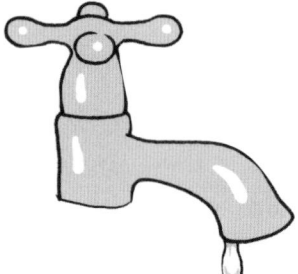

Water is the liquid form of H_2O.

Ice is the solid form of H_2O.

What is the gaseous form of H_2O?

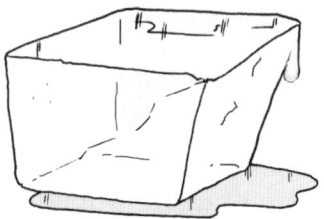

Build your own ice cube

You will need: card
          scissors
          sticky tape
          cling film
          water
          measuring cylinder
          a 12 cm by 12 cm square of plastic
          (cut from a plastic bag)

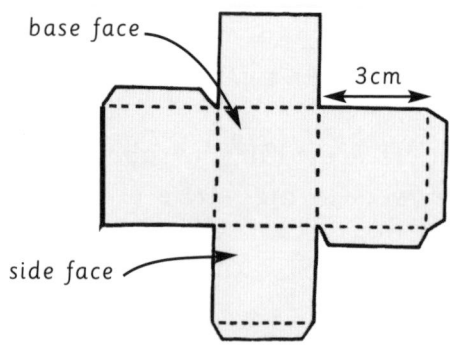

base face

side face

3cm

Method: Measure and cut out carefully the above design on a piece of card to create the net of a cube, minus one face. Make each edge exactly 3cm long.
Fold up four side faces so that they are at right angles to the base face.
Join the four side faces together using sticky tape. You have now made a cube-shaped box. Write your name on the box. Line the inside of your box with plastic so that it will hold water.

With the measurements provided, what volume of water should the box hold?

Pour water into the box, right up to the top, using a measuring cylinder to check how much you pour in. Record the volume of water poured in.

Does this volume match what you predicted? _____

If not, why not? _____

_____

_____

_____

Name: | Date:

Water and ice – sheet B

Place your cube, along with other's, on a tray. Taking care not to spill any water, put the tray in the freezer.

Wait for several hours to ensure that the water has frozen completely.

Remove your ice cube from the freezer, keeping it in the box you made. Observe the ice cube carefully. Describe what you see.

_____

_____

Allow the ice to melt by leaving the box of ice at room temperature.

How long does it take for the ice to melt completely? _____

Describe what you see.

_____

_____

What do you expect the volume of water to be?

Measure and record the volume of water.

Does this volume match what you predicted? _____

If not, why not? _____

_____

You have changed H_2O from water to ice.

Then you allowed the ice to change back to water.

You have <u>reversed</u> the change.

We say that freezing is a reversible change.

Is melting a reversible change? Explain your answer. _____

_____

_____

Name:

Date:

Vocabulary

Match the words to their simple definitions:

reversible   changing from liquid to gaseous form

evaporating   changing from solid to liquid form

dissolving   can be returned to previous state

irreversible   changing from liquid to solid form

melting   changing from gaseous to liquid form

condensing   mixing with water

freezing   cannot be returned to previous state

Opposites puzzle

Across

2. opposite of condensing
5. opposite of reversible
6. opposite of evaporating

Down

1. opposite of freezing
3. opposite of irreversible
4. opposite of melting

Name: | Date:

Evaporation and filtering

Some things can be mixed with water so that they dissolve completely, for example salt will dissolve completely in water. This process is reversible. To retrieve the salt from the water we can make the water evaporate. The salt will be left as a residue.

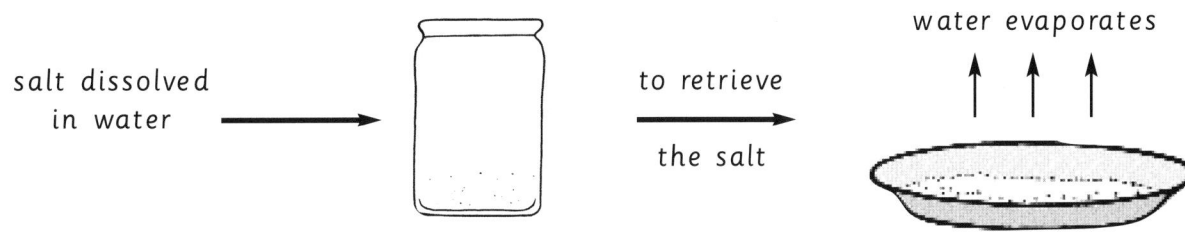

salt dissolved in water →   to retrieve →   the salt   water evaporates

How many words are there in the paragraph above? ☐

Rewrite the main points from the paragraph.
Your summary must have less than 20 words.

_____

_____

_____

Some things can be mixed with water but they do not dissolve, for example sand will not dissolve in water. The particles can still be seen in the water. This mixing process is also reversible. To retrieve the sand from the water we can filter the mixture using paper. The water will run through the filter paper, leaving the sand particles as a residue.

sand particles in the water →   to retrieve →   the sand

How many words are there in the paragraph above? ☐

Rewrite the main points from the paragraph.
Your summary must have less than 20 words.

_____

_____

_____

Name: Date:

Reversible or irreversible?

For each statement, cross out the incorrect word: reversible or irreversible.

1 Melting ice to make water.   reversible/irreversible

2 Mixing sand with water.   reversible/irreversible

3 Boiling an egg.   reversible/irreversible

4 Boiling water to create water vapour.   reversible/irreversible

5 Mixing ingredients to make cakes.   reversible/irreversible

6 Dissolving salt in water.   reversible/irreversible

For each of the changes listed above, explain how it could be reversed <u>or</u> why it cannot be reversed.

(1) _____

_____

_____

(2) _____

_____

_____

(3) _____

_____

(4) _____

_____

(5) _____

_____

(6) _____

_____

_____

Name: Date:

Simply Super Sponges

Ingredients:

2 eggs

100 grams of self-raising flour

100 grams of caster sugar

100 grams of butter (at room temperature)

1 level teaspoon of baking powder

Method:

Pre-heat oven to gas mark 4, 180°C.
Place paper cases in a patty tin.
Put all your ingredients into a mixing bowl.
Use an electric mixer to beat ingredients together for about two minutes.
Put a heaped teaspoon of the mixture into each paper case.
Carefully place the patty tin into the oven.
Leave for fifteen minutes or until golden brown.
Carefully remove from oven.
Leave to cool.

Take care when cooking. The oven is hot!

We show possible curriculum links but we will not have thought of everything so you may like to add some of your own.

Literacy

Vocabulary.
Written explanations of observed effects.
Reading comprehension.
Reading account of investigation written in the third person and using this as a model for children's own writing.

PE

Practical work in forces with throwing and catching, etc.

Art

Link to patterning on high friction surfaces.

History

Understanding the forces of water and air in voyages of exploration.
Link forces to Isaac Newton and understanding of forces to such people as Leonardo da Vinci.

Forces

Numeracy

Recording measurements from forcemeter in newtons.
Interpreting table of results and line graph.
Timing accurately to hundredths of a second.

Worksheet 1 features a cloze test to assess/consolidate understanding of forces. The answers are as follows:
move; direction; friction; easily; equal; upthrust; gravity; magnet; squeezing; forces.

Worksheet 2 is a word puzzle consolidating the vocabulary of forces. The words found should be: upthrust; field; push; friction; weight; handbag; pull; elephant; force; kettle; squeeze; gravity.

Worksheet 3 contains a comprehension exercise about Sir Isaac Newton. This also links to the numeracy work on Worksheet 5.

Worksheet 4 involves writing explanations for the forces in action shown in two pictures. Children should be able to include some of the following ideas in their own sentences:
In picture one, gravity is pulling the boat downward while the upthrust of the water is preventing the boat from sinking. The air is pushing the sail strongly enabling the boat to move forward in the water. The frictional resistance of the water is not enough to prevent this forward motion.
In picture two, the player jumps upwards by pushing with her/his feet on the ground to overcome the force of gravity but gravity will pull her/him back to the ground. Then, friction between the player's foot and the ground will prevent her/him from slipping. The player throws the ball. That push on the ball causes it to move through the air. The air resistance slows it down as it moves and gravity pulls it back towards the earth. If you wish, you could read these explanations to the children before they begin the task, asking them to write them in their own words and providing the following key words on the board: gravity; upthrust; water resistance; friction; air resistance.

Worksheet 5 – numeracy – using a forcemeter to measure in newtons. This sheet also encourages children to look at the 'scale' to see how it is designed. They should find, of course, that the pebble suspended in water weighs less than when it is suspended in air and they may be able to state that the force of gravity is the same but the upthrust of the water has reduced its effect.

Worksheet 6 provides an example of an investigation involving spinners. The account of an actual experiment is written in the third person. Children need to interpret the results and the line graph. Here are some suggested questions and possible answers, though there are many more:

Why are the two sets of results different?
Because human reaction times are different.

Can you see any strange results in either set of data?
Yes, in the first set of data the time goes up when four paperclips are added.

How could we achieve a conclusion if there are inaccuracies in the timing?
By timing several more times and observing overall trends.

Name: _____ Date: _____

Forces vocabulary

Use words from the box to complete the following text. Don't forget to use a capital letter if the word is at the beginning of a sentence.

WORD BANK

equal   upthrust
direction   squeezing   move
friction   magnet   forces
easily   gravity

Forces are what make objects _ _ _ _ , change speed, change _ _ _ _ _ _ _ _ _ ,

change shape or stop. _ _ _ _ _ _ _ _ occurs when two surfaces try to slide against

each other. Two smooth, shiny surfaces may do this _ _ _ _ _ _ . This is known as

low friction. Rougher surfaces, however, provide high friction making the surfaces grip

each other more strongly.

When _ _ _ _ _ forces are exerted on an object it remains still. One example of this

is a ball floating on the water as the _ _ _ _ _ _ _ _ of the water is equal to the

downwards force of _ _ _ _ _ _ _ .

A _ _ _ _ _ _ can exert a force on certain metals causing them to move. Some forces

can cause an object to change shape. An example of this is _ _ _ _ _ _ _ _ _ a

piece of plasticine.

_ _ _ _ _ _ are all around us. Describe the forces can you see in action

in the classroom.

_____

_____

_____

_____

_____

| Across the Curriculum: Science for ages 10–11 | FORCES | | Literacy | 2 |

Name: **Date:**

Hidden words

Begin at space 1. Reading every third letter you will find four words.
Beginning at space 2, reading every third letter you will find four more words.
Beginning at space 3, reading every third letter you will find the final four words.
Write the twelve words you find in the spaces below the puzzle.

¹u	p	e	o	t	i	r	h	g	c	r	h	e	u	t	k	s	h	e	t	a	t	f
²w	i	d	l	e	b	e	l	a	s	d	g	q	p	p	u	u	e	s	l	e	h	l
³f	t	f	e	e	r	l	g	i	e	r	c	p	a	t	h	v	i	a	o	n	t	y

_____ _____ _____

_____ _____ _____

_____ _____ _____

Look at the words you have found.
Split them into two groups – those that concern 'forces' and those that do not.

<u>'Forces' vocabulary</u>

<u>Other vocabulary</u>

Choose words from the 'forces' group to complete the sentence below.

The _ _ _ _ _ known as _ _ _ _ _ _ pulls things towards the earth.

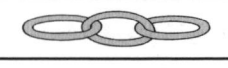
Name: Date:

Sir Isaac Newton

Read this
short text.

Force is measured in **newtons**. These units of
measurement are named after Sir Isaac
Newton who lived from 1642 until 1727. He
was a mathematician and physicist who
became famous for some very important
work. Among his most notable works was his
'law of gravitation'. He was the first person
known to have discovered the law of gravity
and to have written about it.
Now answer these questions.

In what unit is force measured? _____

After whom is this unit of measurement named?

_____

Name one of his most noted works and state what was special about it.

_____

_____

_____

What were the two main subjects that Sir Isaac Newton studied?

_____

_____

Approximately how old was Sir Isaac Newton when he died?

_____

_____

Sir Isaac Newton published three 'laws of motion' in 1687. Using reference books or CD
Roms try to find out exactly what these laws of motion were.

_____

_____

Name: | Date:

Forces in action

In each of the following pictures draw arrows to show forces in action.
Beside each picture give a detailed explanation of the forces you have marked and how
they are affecting the object (or objects) in the picture. Write your explanation in clear
sentences.

Name: Date:

Using forcemeters

On each of the pictures, mark the scale in the same way that your forcemeter is marked.

Use your forcemeter to weigh each of the following objects:

a large pebble
a book
a whiteboard marker

Look at your forcemeter carefully and record the measurements on the scales shown below, for each of the objects.

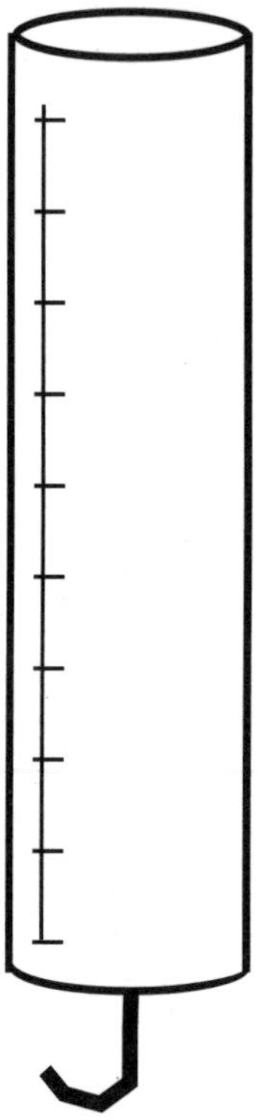

The pebble weighs

_____

newtons.

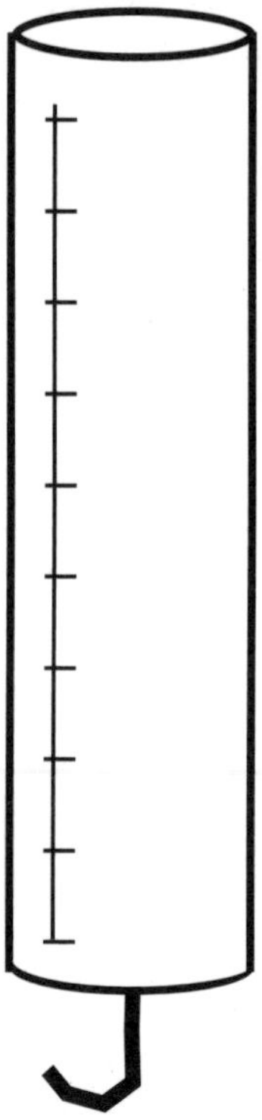

The book weighs

_____

newtons.

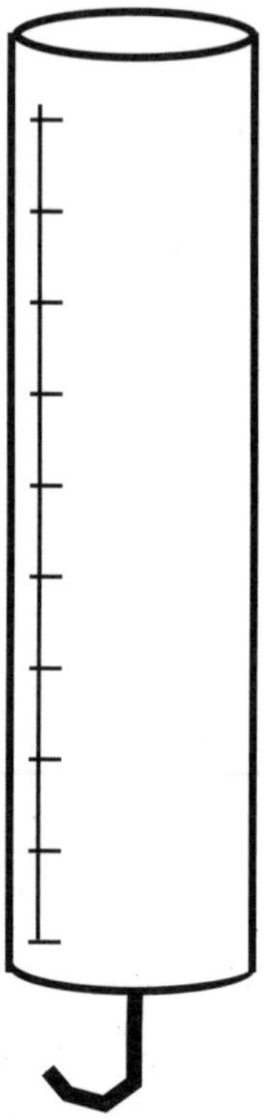

The whiteboard marker weighs

_____

newtons.

Now suspend the pebble from the forcemeter again, but this time in water.

Record the pebble's weight again and copy the scale from the forcemeter.

The pebble in water weighs

_____

newtons.

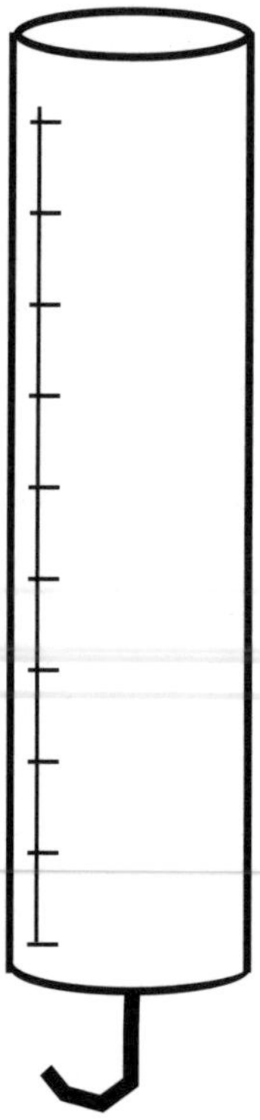

Is the measurement in water the same as it was in the air? _____

Try to explain this.

_____

_____

_____

_____

_____

_____

_____

_____

Name: Date:

Spinner investigation

Objective
To investigate the effect of gravity as a downward force compared to air resistance as an upward force.

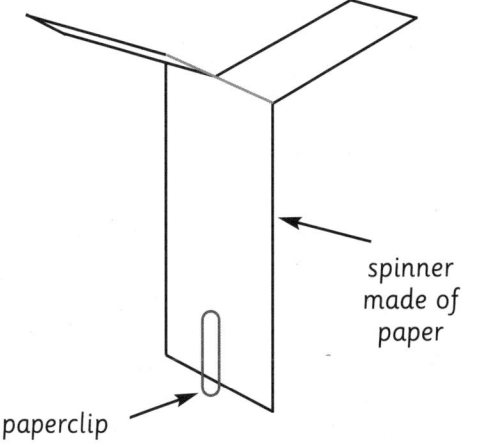

spinner made of paper

paperclip

Method
A spinner was dropped from a height of 2.5 metres and timed to an accuracy of hundredths of seconds by two people using electronic stopwatches.
A paperclip was attached to the spinner and it was dropped and timed again.
This was repeated with two paperclips, then three, four, five and six.

Results

number of paperclips	0	1	2	3	4	5	6
time recorded on stopwatch A	2.03	1.84	1.72	1.41	1.44	1.18	1.17
time recorded on stopwatch B	1.92	1.74	1.50	1.29	1.28	1.26	1.01

These results were plotted on a line graph.

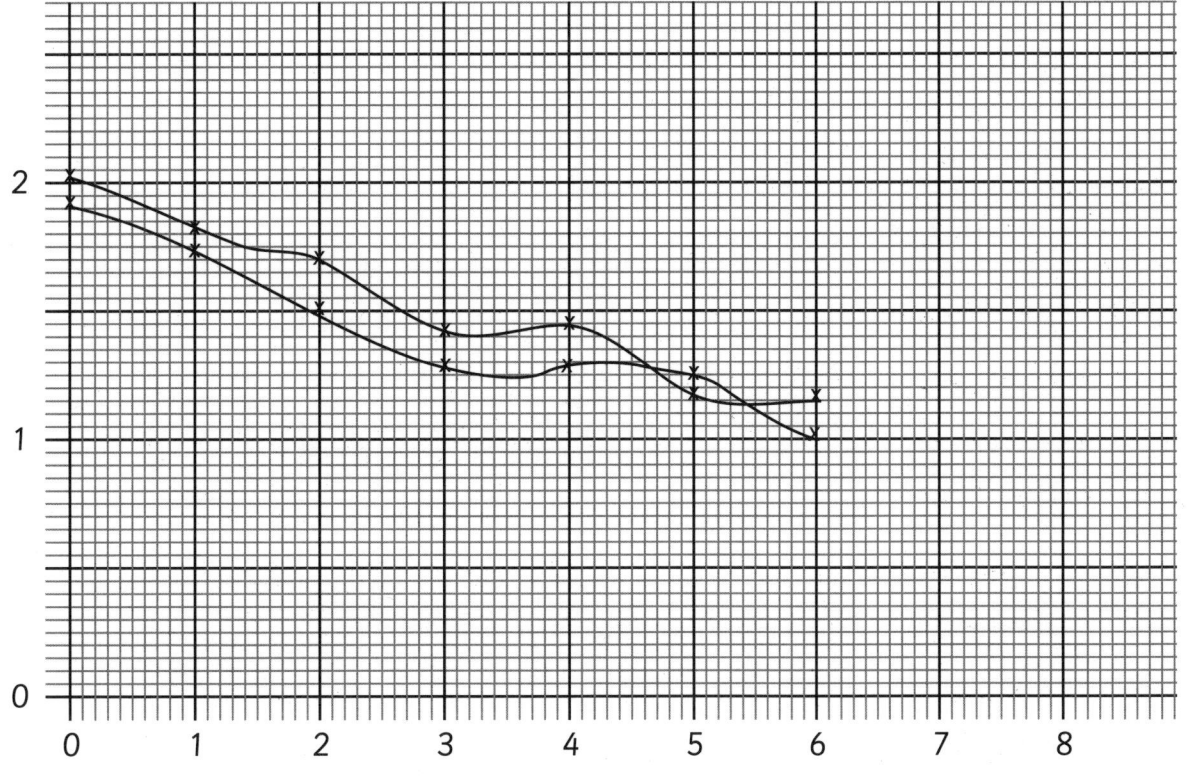

Discuss the results. Your teacher will have some questions for you.
You could try the investigation yourself.

We show possible curriculum links but we will not have thought of everything so you may like to add some of your own.

Literacy

Following clues to find cloze words. Putting these words into context. Following instructions.

DT

'Up periscope!' based on structures.

Art

Still life 'reflecting'.

How We See Things

Numeracy

Measuring acute and obtuse angles. Observing that angles on a straight line add up to 180°. Entering data into a table.

Worksheets 1 and 2 satisfy the literacy requirement to extend vocabulary through word games and reinforce the scientific learning implicit in this topic.
The answers are as follows.

Worksheet 1: opaque; shadow; reflector.
Worksheet 2: source; moon; transparent.

Worksheet 3 works on measuring angles and reinforces the idea that the angle of incidence is equal to the angle of reflection. The answers are as follows.

Example, a and b both equal 45°
1 a and b both equal 60°
2 a and b both equal 20°
3 a and b both equal 75°
4 a and b both equal 35°

Worksheet 4 continues this theme while introducing the idea that angles on a straight line always add up to 180°. The answers are as follows.

Example, a, b and c all equal 60°
1 a and b both equal 25°, c equals 130°
2 a and b both equal 55°, c equals 70°
3 a and b both equal 85°, c equals 10°

Worksheet 5 encourages children to consider the properties necessary for reflection and should generate a considerable amount of discussion.

Worksheet 6 contains a DT task that complements the objectives contained within the structures unit.

Art
Although we have not included a Worksheet for this, the requirement to do a still life picture lends itself to this topic – a collection of objects for drawing/painting could include some reflective items adding a dimension of interest to the artwork produced.

Name:

Date:

Riddles

Solve the riddles and discover the science.

My first is in boy but never in girl. _____

My second is found at the front of a pearl. _____

My third is in any, but never in none. _____

My fourth is in quiz, quest and question. _____

My fifth's not in black but is found in blue. _____

My last you will find standing twice in a queue. _____

An _ _ _ _ _ _ object will not allow light to pass through.

My first is in fish and also in sea. _____

My second is found in who, him and he. _____

My third is in snake, and also in ladder. _____

My next's not in merry but is seen in sadder. _____

My fifth is in stop and also in go. _____

My sixth's not in fast but is found in slow. _____

When light is blocked a _ _ _ _ _ _ is formed.

My first is in star but not in the sun. _____

My next is in three and also in one. _____

The third you will find in a foot not a knee. _____

The fourth is in lock but not in the key. _____

Next is a vowel but not a, o or u. _____

The sixth letter is both in chomp and in chew. _____

The next letter sounds like a meal you might eat. _____

The eighth is in sofa but not found in seat. _____

My last is in stare but not within sight. _____

The mirror is a good _ _ _ _ _ _ _ _ _ _ of light.

Can you make a science riddle for a friend to do?

Andrew Brodie Publications © A & C Black Publishers Ltd.

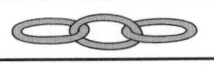
Name:

Date:

More riddles

Solve the riddles

My first is in sheep but not in lamb. _____

My next is in lorry but not in a tram. _____

My third is between letters t and v. _____

My fourth is in dinner but not in my tea. _____

My fifth is in clock, clean, clam and clown. _____

My last is in headdress but not in a crown. _____

The sun is a light _ _ _ _ _ _ _ .

My first is in both my and mouth. _____

My second found in north and south. _____

My third is seen in fork and spoon. _____

My last is in both song and tune. _____

The _ _ _ _ reflects light from the sun.

My first is in meat but not in meal. _____

My second's in run but not in kneel. _____

My third is in rabbit and also in cat. _____

My fourth is in standing but not found in sat. _____

My fifth is in fish but not in chip. _____

My sixth's not in boats but is found in ships. _____

My next is in sparrow and also in hawk. _____

My eighth is in chair but not found in seat. _____

My ninth is in seven, eight, nine and ten. _____

My tenth will be found in both now and again. _____

My last is to be seen in truth, tell and true. _____

A clear thing now find that lets light shine right through.

A _ _ _ _ _ _ _ _ _ _ _ object will allow light to pass through.

Name: Date:

Measuring angles 1

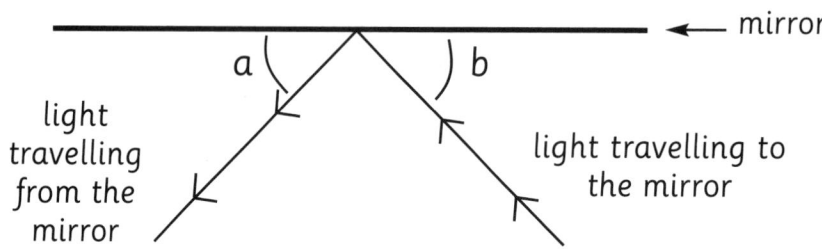

Look at the diagrams below – use a protractor to measure the angles marked **a** and **b** on each diagram.

1

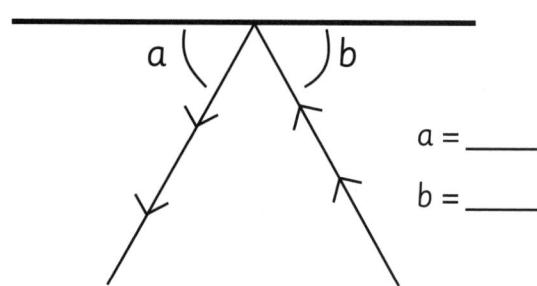

a = _____

b = _____

2

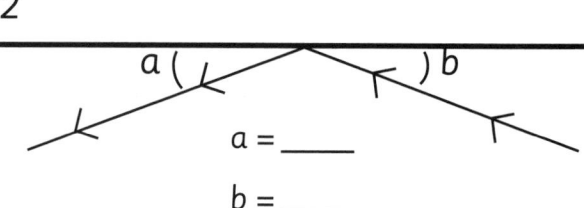

a = _____

b = _____

3

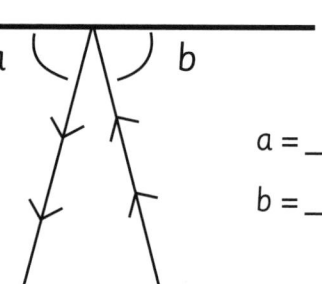

a = _____

b = _____

4

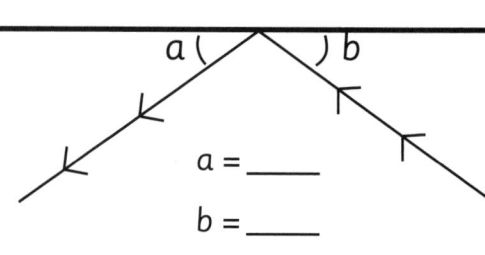

a = _____

b = _____

Did you notice anything about the angles you measured?
Use the lines below to write what you found out.

_____

_____

_____

Name:

Date:

Measuring angles 2

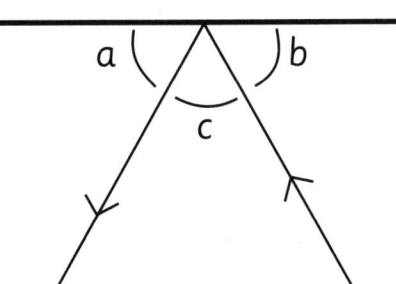

On Worksheet 3 you discovered that angle **a** is always equal to angle **b**.

On this sheet you also need to measure angle **c**.

On each diagram you are also asked to add together angles **a**, **b** and **c**.

1

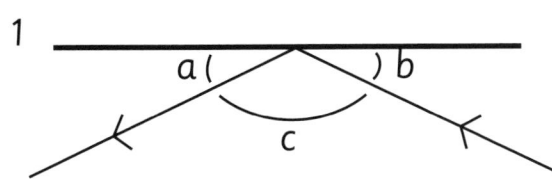

a = _____

b = _____

c = _____

total a + b + c = _____

2

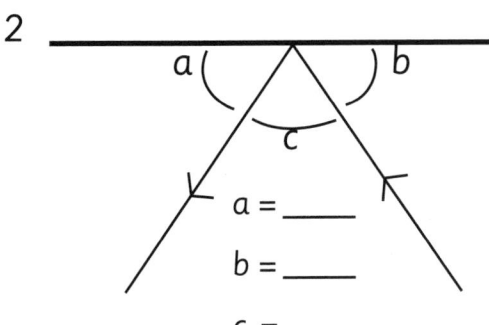

a = _____

b = _____

c = _____

total a + b + c = _____

3

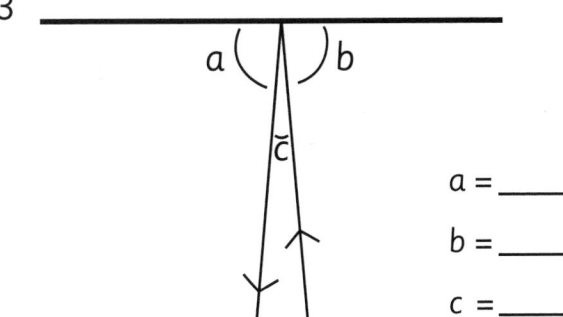

a = _____

b = _____

c = _____

total a + b + c = _____

What did you notice this time? Write your answer below.

_____

_____

_____

HOW WE SEE THINGS

Numeracy

Name: Date:

Reflections

You will need: a torch

eight items (such as a ruler, a shoe, a mirror, a biscuit tin lid, this Worksheet, a spoon, a mug)

List your items in the left hand column of the table below. In the next column give each item a score, according to how well you think it will reflect your face or a beam of light from the torch. Give a score of 8 for the best reflector and 1 for the least successful reflector. Test each item, then give it a score based on your observations.

Item	Predicted reflectivity score	Actual reflectivity score

Were your predictions correct?

Explain your results by making a general statement about how effective some things are at reflecting according to how shiny they are.

Name:

Date:

Up periscope!

Work with a partner.

Your task is to make a viewing instrument to help you see over walls or round corners.

Your viewing instrument should be **easily portable**, **robust** enough for everyday use and be fit for use in **rainy weather.**

Your viewing instrument should have at least one moving part. This might help you to get a better view!

Design your instrument with care.

Draw and label your design in the box below.

We show possible curriculum links but we will not have thought of everything so you may like to add some of your own.

Literacy

Vocabulary development using appropriate definitions. Writing in sentences to answer questions related to electrical safety and circuits.

History

How life was different before electricity – linked to history topic. Children could consider the difference in the number of electrical items found in a home in the 1940s and today.

Geography

When undertaking 'investigating rivers' or 'mountain environments', look for the water flow being used to generate energy.

Changing Circuits

Numeracy

Presenting results in graphs.

Worksheet 1 contains literacy work on the vocabulary of electricity and is designed to ensure understanding of vocabulary. An element of alphabetical order is built into this work.

Worksheet 2 features literacy work answering questions using knowledge of electrical circuits and electrical safety. Children are also asked to draw a scientific diagram of an electrical circuit.

The answer to the first question should indicate the dangerous nature of mains electricity and the safety of low voltage batteries.
The second question requires children to state that the plastic on the wire is an insulator and that touching the bare wire will cause an electric shock.
The circuit shown will result in the bulb
lighting up as a complete circuit has been made.
The circuit diagram should be similar to this:

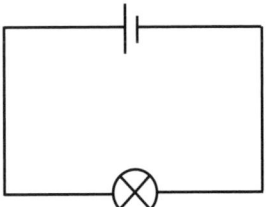

Worksheet 3 is a literacy sheet encouraging children to consider what they know about changing circuits. The sentence should read: The shorter wire will light the bulb more brightly. Theoretically a bulb will light more brightly by using shorter wires as the resistance in the wires will be less than if longer wires are used. However, in using materials in the classroom there may not be an observable difference. This provides an ideal opportunity for an investigation that children could carry out using the same circuit as shown on Worksheet 2.

Worksheets 4 and 5 focus on the use of electricity in the home. Children need to interpret the results of the information given, finding the 'mean' of a set of numbers and the range of results. The number of children chosen for the chart was twelve, so a natural progression would be to construct simple pie charts for the four colour coded ranges of results within the bar chart. These sheets also promote discussion about items powered by mains electricity in the home and could form the basis for similar surveys to be carried out about children's own homes. The answers are as follows.

Initial of child	A	B	C	D	E	F	G	H	I	J	K	L
Number of appliances	36	47	42	62	50	28	46	56	44	37	30	50

Total = 528; Dan; The watch is not powered by mains electricity;
Fran with 28; Ella was correct; The range of results is 34.

Revision pages
The three puzzle pages form the basis for some revision and consolidation work covering the main areas of key stage 2 science. To complete the puzzles the children may find it helpful to refer to revision sheet 4.

Revision sheet 4 could be used at any stage during the school year or simply for revision at the end of the year. The list of scientific vocabulary could be copied into exercise books to enable children to construct their own glossary of scientific terms.

Name: Date:

Electricity vocabulary

Arrange the words from the box in alphabetical order on the lines down the left-hand side of the page. By each word give a clear definition.

Remember that while some words have more than one meaning, your definition must refer to its electrical meaning, for example current will not mean 'up to date' and 'cell' will have nothing to do with a prison!

> ### WORD BANK
>
> current   insulator   circuit
>
> electricity   conductor   cell

Name: Date:

Electricity circuits

● Use your scientific knowledge to answer these questions.

● Write your answers in clear sentences.

Why do you carry out electrical experiments in school using batteries rather than using mains electricity?

_____

_____

_____

You are about to plug in the television when you notice a small cut in the plastic coating of the lead and a tiny amount of wire is visible. Should you still plug it in? Explain your answer fully.

_____

_____

_____

You have made the circuit shown. Will the bulb light up? Give reasons for your answer.

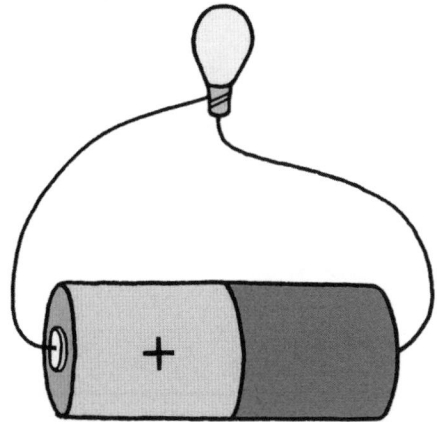

_____

_____

_____

_____

_____

_____

_____

In the box on the right, draw the correct circuit diagram to represent the circuit shown above.

Use:

   straight lines for the wires

   this symbol for a bulb   ⊗

   this symbol for a battery   ⊣⊢

CHANGING CIRCUITS

Name:

Date:

Balloon words

Each balloon below contains the letters of a word.
Find out what each word is and use them to complete the sentence at the bottom of the page. This sentence answers the question correctly.

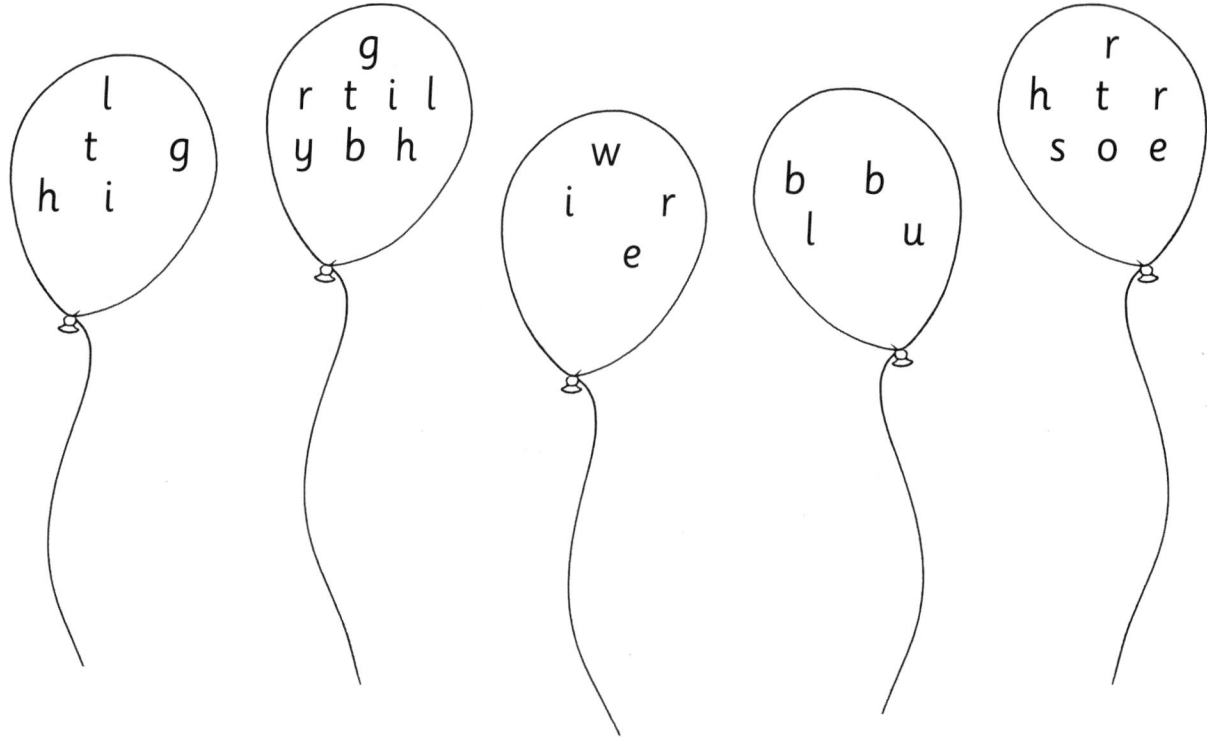

You are making a bulb light in a simple circuit. You have a choice of two pieces of wire to use, one is longer than the other. Which piece of wire will make the bulb shine more brightly?

The _____ _____ will _____ the _____

more _____ .

Is the sentence you have just written true? Draw the diagram for a circuit that you could use to test this theory.

Use:

   straight lines for the wires

   this symbol for a bulb   ⊗

   this symbol for a battery   ⊦⊦

Carry out the test to see if the theory is correct.

Name: | Date:

Electrical appliances in the home

Twelve children were asked to count the number of mains electrical appliances in their homes. Their results are shown below.

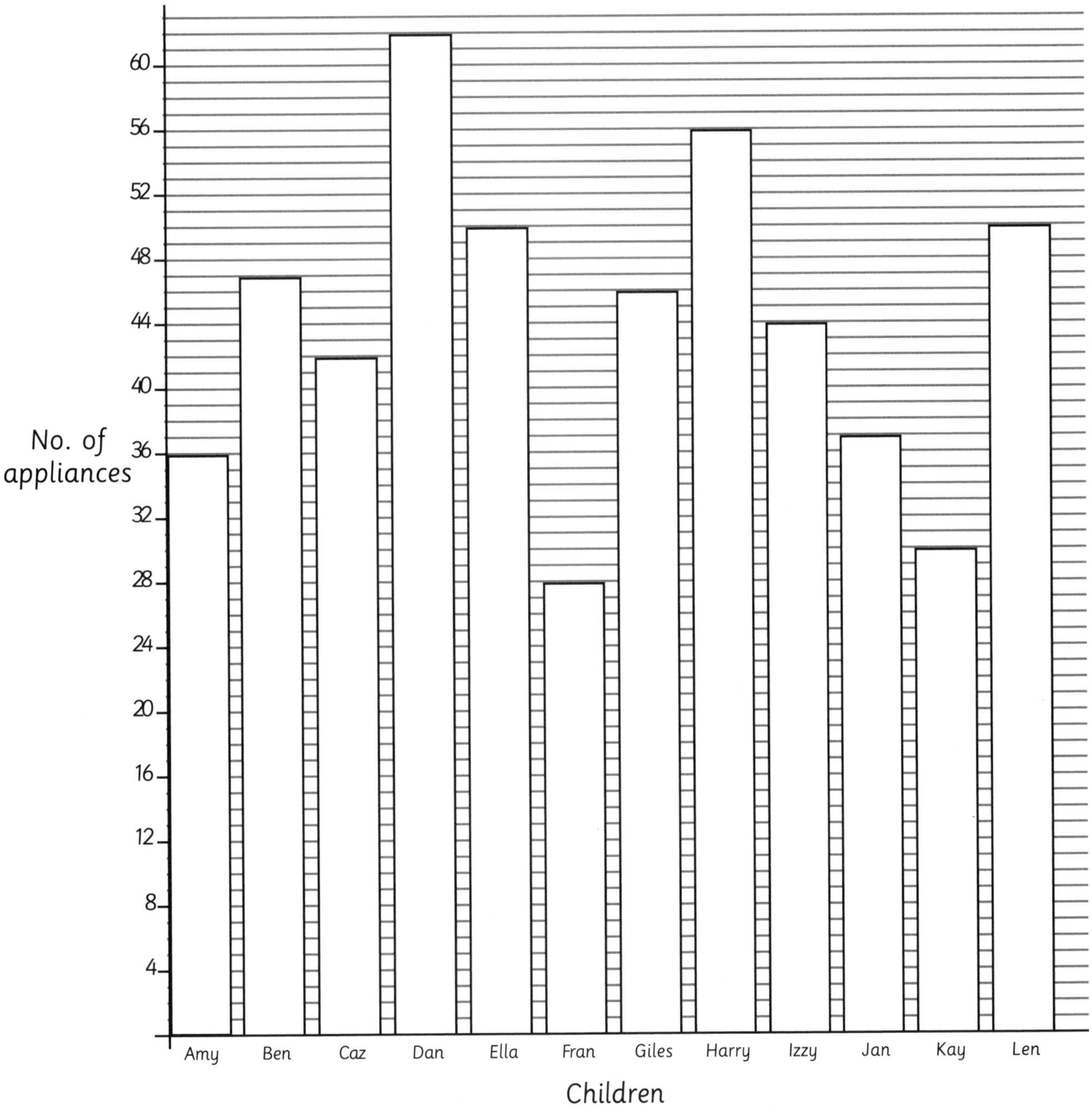

No. of appliances

Bar chart showing number of appliances for children: Amy 36, Ben 47, Caz 42, Dan 62, Ella 50, Fran 28, Giles 46, Harry 56, Izzy 44, Jan 37, Kay 30, Len 50

Children

Colour the box chart as follows:

Red – all bars showing less than 40 appliances.

Green – all bars showing between 40 and 49 appliances.

Yellow – all bats showing between 50 and 59 appliances.

Blue – all bars with 60 or more appliances.

Now answer the questions on Worksheet 5.

Name: Date:

Mean and range

Answer these questions about the bar graph on Worksheet 4.

Use the data from the bar chart to complete this table.

Initial of child												
Number of appliances												

Add together all the data for the 'number of appliances'. _____

Who counted more than 60 electrical appliances in their home? _____

Amy asked if her battery powered wristwatch should be added to her graph. What do you think the answer to that question should be? Explain your answer.

_____

_____

_____

Who counted the lowest number of appliances in their home and how many did they find? _____

The teacher asked the twelve children to find the **mean** average number of appliances. She explained that this was to be done by adding all of the results together and dividing the answer by the number of children (12). Do this yourself.

Amy thought the <u>mean</u> was 42.
Giles thought the <u>mean</u> was 43.8.
Ella thought the <u>mean</u> was 44.

Who was right? _____

What is the difference between the lowest and highest results on the bar chart? _____
This result is known as the range.

Name: | Date:

Scientific vocabulary

Try to find the missing words for the puzzle below, then write good clues to go with each answer. You may need a science book or dictionary to help you.

Clues down

1. _____

_____

_____

_____

2. _____

_____

_____

5. _____

_____

_____

7. _____

_____

_____

1. V _ G _ T _ _ _ _ S
E
R
_
_
_
3. A _ T _ R I _ S
L
T I
E _
4. S T _ G _ A
O
6. C _ _ _ D _ N S A T _ _ N
C
8. F _ R _ _ M _ _ R

Clues across

1. _____

_____

3. _____

_____

4. _____

_____

6. _____

_____

8. _____

_____

Name: Date:

Scientific vocabulary

The first one has been done for you.

In the first column is a word that rhymes with the answer to the clue.

In the second column is the 'clue'.

Write the answer in the third column.

Rhyming words	Clues	Answers
stay	A creature hunted for food by another	prey
one	This light source is our nearest star	
mirth	Our planet	
perm	A micro-organism	
lanes	These carry blood to the heart	
addiction	A force that might stop you slipping	
hire us	These can make you feel ill – also a term for harm spread among computers	
lass	Not solid or liquid	
mistrust	A force found in water	
boot	Eat this as part of a healthy diet	

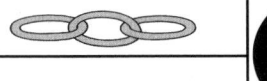
Name: Date:

Scientific vocabulary

Choose scientific words to correctly fill in the spaces below.

Our _ _ _ _ _   _ _ _ _ _ _ consists of planets that orbit the sun.

A _ _ _ _ _ _ _ _ _ _ _ object allows light to partially pass through it.

_ _ _ _ _ _ _ _ carry blood away from the heart.

When water becomes water vapour it is known as _ _ _ _ _ _ _ _ _ _ _ _ .

The force of _ _ _ _ _ _ _ _ pulls things towards the earth.

The _ _ _ _ _ _ _ _ _ is the framework of bones that gives our bodies support and protects our _ _ _ _ _ _ and other internal organs.

A _ _ _ _ _ _ _ _ is a complete route through which electricity can flow.

All matter is in one of three forms _ _ _ _ _ _ , _ _ _ _ _ _ or _ _ _ .

Now choose three more words to do some sentence puzzles for a friend to complete.

_____

_____

_____

_____

_____

_____

_____

_____

_____

_____

_____

Name:

Date:

Science terms you should know

absorbent	germ	sepal
air resistance	gravity	shadow
arteries	habitat	skeleton
attract	heart	Solar System
blood	ice	solid
boiling	incisor	solution
canine	insulator	source
circuit	life cycle	sphere
component	liquid	sun
condensation	melt	stamen
conductor	molar	stigma
consumer	moon	temperature
darkness	opaque	thermometer
daylight	orbit	translucent
diet	organism	transparent
dissolve	oxygen	upthrust
earth	petal	vegetables
electrical	pollen	veins
evaporation	predator	vertebrate
flexible	prey	vibration
force	producers	virus
forcemeter	pulse	water cycle
freeze	reflector	water vapour
friction	repel	
fruit	reproduction	
gas	rotate	

Andrew Brodie Publications © A & C Black Publishers Ltd.